Living In Another Time

WORKING IN THE FIRST FACTORIES

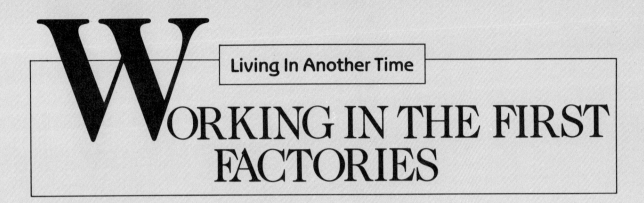

W

Living In Another Time

ORKING IN THE FIRST FACTORIES

Illustrations by Ginette Hoffmann
Text by Patrice Coupry
Translated by Christopher Sharp

Silver Burdett Company
Morristown, New Jersey and Agincourt, Ontario

For my parents,
Ginette Hoffmann

Series coordinated by Michel Pierre
in collaboration with Elisabeth Sebaoun

English text consultant:
Francis W. Wcislo,
Assistant Professor of History,
Vanderbilt University

Library of Congress Cataloging-in-Publication Data

Coupry, Patrice.
    Working in the first factories.

    (Living in another time)
    Translation of: Au temps des premières usines.
    Summary: Nine-year-old Louise lives with her family in a
nineteenth century coal mining community and observes changes
taking place as new factories emerge and the miners rebel against
their harsh working conditions. Sections of the story alternate with
brief factual information on aspects of working conditions in mines
and early factories.
    1. Coal mines and mining—Europe—Juvenile literature. 2.
Industry—History—Juvenile literature. [1. Coal mines and mining—
Fiction. 2. Industry—History—Fiction] I. Hoffmann, Ginette, ill. II.
Title. III. Series: Des enfants dans l'histoire. English.
PZ7.C83135Wo 1986   [Fic]   86-6746
ISBN 0-382-09178-7

Published pursuant to an agreement with Casterman, Paris
First published in French by Casterman as *Des enfants dans L'Histoire:
Au temps des premieres usines*

First published in the United States in 1986
by Silver Burdett Company
Morristown, New Jersey

Published simultaneously in Canada
by GLC/Silver Burdett Publishers

Table of Contents

Page

Coal Country 7
    School One Hundred Years Ago 11

Down in the Mine 13
    A Short History of Coal 17

The Accident 19
    Children at Work in the Mines 23

Iron and Steel Making 25
    The Blast Furnace 31

Building Metal Monsters 33
    From the *Rocket* to the TGV 37

The Strike 39
    May 1st 43

Mines of Today 44
Places to Write for More Information 45
Important Dates 46

Coal Country

It was a cold April afternoon, and the small town lay covered by gray clouds. Spring did not seem to want to come. The miners' and factory workers' small houses looked very sad and dreary.

Coal dust clung everywhere—to walls, clothes, and newly opened leaves on the trees. Two women walked along the street with pale, sickly-looking children by their sides. Their husbands worked at the mine or in factory workshops and would not be home until dusk.

As usual, when school let out at four-thirty, Louise was the first to leave the classroom. She was in a hurry to get out to her mother, who was waiting for her at the school gate. Louise was only nine years old, but she seemed older because of her serious-looking face.

"Mother, I got the best grade in spelling."

"That's wonderful, my dear, I'm very proud of you."

Louise's mother, Jeanne, was very happy when her daughter received good grades in school. When she was Louise's age, she had not been given the chance to go to school. Every evening, Jeanne watched her daughter do her homework and listened to her repeat her lessons.

Jeanne took her child's hand, and they both started off toward home. Together they walked along the cobblestone streets. On their way they passed in front of brick houses that all seemed very much alike. The front of each house had two windows with wooden shutters. In the backyard there was a small garden, where the miners grew vegetables and fruit. Many of the gardens had small sheds for storing tools and a hutch for raising rabbits. Sometimes there were even a few chickens and a pig.

"What time will Father be home?" Louise asked, looking at her mother.

"He'll be home before dark, I think. But today, he's expecting your Uncle Julien for dinner."

Louise's father, Paul, and her uncle, Julien, were miners. Like hundreds of others, they came home in the evening dirty and exhausted, their faces covered with black coal dust.

As she walked home with her mother, Louise thought about her father working hundreds of feet

beneath the ground. Although she knew it was silly, she wished she could see through the ground, down to where her father was working. He was probably in a tunnel, digging coal with a pick by the light of a safety lamp.

Louise and her mother finally arrived in front of their house. Jeanne opened the door. She looked at Louise and said, "Now, wipe your shoes on the doormat before taking them off. I just waxed the kitchen and bedroom floors this afternoon."

Jeanne went to the kitchen. She unpacked her grocery basket. There were potatoes, turnips, bacon, and lard. As she began peeling the vegetables, Louise came and sat down to do her homework. This was a time she particularly liked because everything was so peaceful. The only sound she could hear was the crackling of the fire in the wood stove. It was used not only for cooking but also for heating the room.

When Jeanne finished making supper, she sat down next to Louise to mend some clothes. Slowly the light grew dimmer. Jeanne suddenly realized she was working in the dark and got up to light the gas lamp. As she lit the lamp, she exclaimed, "Your father should be home any minute now! I'd better hurry and heat some water for his bath. Louise, please fetch the tub and soap for me."

The tub was an old barrel Paul used each evening to wash himself in. He had to get rid of all the dirt and coal dust from a hard day's work.

School One Hundred Years Ago

In France, in 1882, a law declared that school would be free for boys and girls from age 6 to 13. From then on, all those children had to go to school. This law is what made it possible for Louise to go to school. Her parents, though, had hardly learned to read or write.

A hundred years ago, classrooms were big rooms with high ceilings. Desks were placed next to each other and lined up in rows. There were two to five children in each row.

On top of their desks, the pupils had earthenware inkwells, in which they dipped their quill pens, and a groove for storing the pens when they were not being used. They also used slates and chalk to do their writing and arithmetic exercises.

Down in the Mine

In white earthenware bowls, Jeanne served the vegetable soup and the pieces of bacon. Paul took the knife he always kept with him from his pocket. He used it to cut large slices of bread for everyone to dip in the thick broth.

After dinner, Paul and Julien lit their pipes and sat back to discuss their favorite subject—the mine.

Julien was a *kibbler*. At the bottom of the shaft, he guided his inseparable companion who pulled small vehicles, called *tubs*, loaded with over six hundred pounds of coal. The companion's name was Lucky.

"A mighty fine horse!" Julien exclaimed. I remember when Andre, the blacksmith, brought him down into the mine two years ago. Lucky's eyes were covered with leather blinkers, and his legs were strapped together. He was suspended from a chain and slowly lowered down the shaft. He was terrified. I remember it very well, because afterwards it took me awhile to calm him down. I had to pet him gently and say soft words to make him stop shaking. Since then, he has saved my life many times. He senses danger before I do. He'll refuse to go into a *gallery* (a tunnel from which coal is mined) if he thinks it might collapse.

13

Louise would have liked to have seen Lucky, but that was not possible. Once horses went down into the mine, they never came back up. They never saw daylight again! But their underground stables were kept clean. They were also fed plenty of oats and hay.

The shaft where Lucky had gone down was used every day by hundreds of miners. They went down in huge iron cages that were attached to sturdy cables. The same shaft was used to bring up the heavy tubs loaded with coal dug from the earth.

A narrower shaft was used to bring air into the mine. It also was used as an emergency exit, if necessary. There were long iron ladders attached to the shaft's brick walls, making it possible for the miners to climb up and down.

Between these two shafts, the galleries began. They ran alongside the *seams* of coal. In this underground maze of tunnels, men deep down in the earth worked with safety lamps attached to their wide-brimmed leather hats. These lamps were sometimes called their "third eye." The suffocating heat forced the miners to work without their shirts. They had little protection from the sharp edges of the hard rock.

Digging a gallery was not easy work. First, dynamite was used to break away the rock. A *linstock* (a staff to which a match could be attached) allowed the miner to light the explosives from a safe distance away. When the rubble was cleared out, timbermen moved in to "timber" the newly made space. They installed wooden beams to prop up the ceiling so that it would not collapse. The

miners then used picks to break the coal loose from the seams. Then it was loaded into tubs that horses pulled along railtracks.

Each load was hoisted from the mine and taken to a coal-preparation plant. There, in a big wooden shed, the coal was emptied onto a sliding surface. As it rolled down, women and young girls sorted the coal with rakes, shovels, and sometimes even their hands. It was their job to remove stones and debris. The coal was then sent to the blast furnace.

Jeanne had done that job for a long time, even after giving birth to Emile and Gustave, Louise's older brothers. After a while, though, she stopped. She was too tired and wanted to raise her children and take care of the house.

Every evening when Louise looked at her father, she felt both fear and pride. It frightened her to think of the danger he faced in his job. Yet she knew it was a job that required strength, courage, and intelligence.

Every miner knew that he could easily be injured, be caught in an accident, or fall prey to disease. A forty-year-old miner often looked like a much older man. His skin was covered with scars, and worst of all, his lungs had *silicosis*, a disease caused by coal dust.

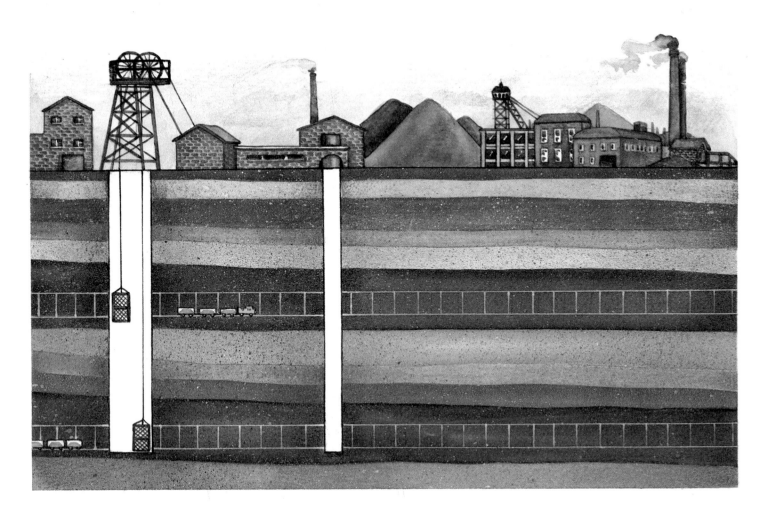

A Short History of Coal

Coal was formed ~~millions~~ _{thousands} of years ago. When large forests died, they left thick layers of matter on the ground. In certain areas these layers were eventually covered by the sea. The matter began to rot and slowly formed a hard black substance called coal.

Around 1750, thanks to coal, many industries began to develop, especially the iron industry. Coal could also be used to heat houses, and fuel the steam engines which made trains and ships run.

Of all the many grades of coal, *anthracite* is the most sought after. This is because it gives off more heat than any other grade.

The Accident

Jeanne didn't say much during the meal. She listened and made sure that everyone had enough to eat.

Suddenly the meal was interrupted by loud knocking at the door. When Jeanne jumped up to open it, in walked Jacques, a miner from the night shift. Sweat ran down his face and left white lines on his mask of coal dust. He was out of breath but managed to blurt out the news that Paul and Julien had already seen written on his face.

"There's been an . . . an accident . . . in the new gallery. The roof caved in, and timbers and large rocks fell on the men . . . about ten of them are trapped down there . . ."

Before Jacques had even finished the story, Paul and Julien had jumped to their feet. Quickly, they grabbed their capes, slipped on their wooden shoes, and jammed their wide-brimmed hats on their heads.

"Father, I want to go with you," Louise said.

"No, no. You stay here Louise. We may be gone for some time. We'll be back as soon as possible."

19

The three men hurried along the dark streets toward the mine. By the time they arrived, many people were already gathered around. Relatives and friends of the trapped men joined the workers at the mine. There were the coal-tram conductors, the tippers who emptied the cars, and the davymen who distributed the "third eye" to the miners. No one spoke. Women grasped their handkerchiefs and silently wept.

Paul immediately went to ask about the situation.

"Part of the group has stayed below to start clearing away the rubble," the engineer said. "Three firemen have gone down with breathing equipment."

Since volunteers were needed, Paul and Julien joined a group of timbermen who were getting ready to enter the mine. The ride down the shaft seemed endless. When they came to the bottom, things were not as bad as they had feared. It was only the entrance to the gallery that had collapsed and not the gallery itself. There did not seem to be any danger of flooding or of a *firedamp* explosion. (This kind of explosion is caused by a buildup of mine gas that blows up at the slightest spark.) Nevertheless, speed was still of great importance—the trapped miners were running out of air.

Very cautiously the miners began to clear away the large rocks that blocked the opening to the gallery. Suddenly, the miners heard a noise. It was a black-nosed, shiny-eyed rat with sharp white teeth. There were thousands of rats that lived in the galleries, feeding on the scraps the miners left behind from their lunches. The rat darted off at the sight of the men. It was a sign of hope!

"If that rat was able to survive the accident, the trapped men must also be alive!" Julien exclaimed.

Paul waved his arms for everyone to be quiet. He took off his hat and put his ear against the wall.

"Hey! I hear voices, they're alive."

The rescuers dug frantically. The trapped miners shouted, hoping to be heard.

After two hours of feverish work, the rescuers finally reached the unfortunate men. Out of the ten who had been trapped in the gallery, only one was dead. A timber had fallen on him and crushed his kidneys. Some of the other men had broken arms or legs, and three had no serious injuries at all.

It was almost daylight when the survivors and the rescuers came to the surface. Several men carried the broken body, and others helped the injured.

Children at Work in the Mines

Up until around 1880, young children worked in mines. Often they had to work from a young age because their families were so poor. Because of their small size, they were able to crawl through the lowest galleries. They pushed trams loaded with coal. If their strength gave way, they risked being crushed.

They were exposed to the same dangers as adults and lived in horrible conditions. Some were already at work by the young age of six.

In 1861, in Bethune, France, eighteen people were killed in a mine accident. Seven were children; some were only nine years old.

Iron and Steel Making

Men were busy working at the bottom of the blast furnace. They were filling buckets up with iron ore or roasted coal, known as *coke*.

Louise's older brother Gustave worked with these men. He watched as a loaded bucket was lifted to the top of the blast furnace. There the iron ore in it was dumped into the opening.

Day and night, iron ore and coke were fed into the hungry monster. After each layer of iron ore was added, a layer of coke had to be added to keep the furnace burning. The temperature had to rise to over 2400 degrees Fahrenheit to make a mixture of iron containing a small amount of carbon. This ran off at the bottom of the furnace and traveled through channels of sand and into molds. With a shovelful of sand ready, the sweaty men kept an eye on the river of molten pig iron to make sure it did not overflow.

Once the iron was cooled, it could be used to make pots, pipes, and stoves. It was heavy and hard but had one serious drawback. The carbon in it made it very brittle.

It wasn't until the end of the nineteenth century that a process was developed to remove the carbon from the iron. The end product of this process is the metal known as *steel*. Steel is a very solid metal and is easy to work with. Items such as sheet metal, rails, and beams are made from steel and used to build bridges, ships, and trains. It is even used to make nuts and bolts!

The carbon in the iron can be removed by using a huge bowl-shaped receptacle called a *converter*. The metal is placed in the converter and heated to 2900 degrees Fahrenheit. When it reaches that temperature, the carbon turns into a gas and evaporates.

Suddenly a shrill-sounding bell announced the end of work for the day shift. Gustave hurried out. He did not want to keep Louise waiting in front of the gate. On Saturday afternoons Louise often went to the town where her two brothers worked to visit with them. First she went and waited for Gustave. Then together they would go to meet their brother Emile where he worked. On Saturday evenings the boys brought Louise home and spent some time with their parents.

"Hello, Gustave," she said, giving him a kiss. "How are you?"

"My back hurts, but work must go on. Say, I heard there was some trouble last night. Was there an accident?"

"Yes, a tunnel collapsed on some miners. One of them died. Father spent the whole night down there. He'll tell you all about it when we get home."

28

One of the first power hammers, in 1840

Together they walked away from the buildings where the blast furnace was. As they walked, they passed the ironworks with its huge brick chimneys. The chimneys were so tall that they seemed to scrape the sky. From time to time, a hissing sound could be heard, followed by a loud crashing noise. This was the power hammer, a gigantic machine that stood 65 feet high and weighed over 100 tons.

"These past few days," Gustave said to his sister, "the power hammer workers have been forging a propeller shaft for a steamboat. I think it's the biggest piece of metal they've ever worked on. They heated it in the forge until it was red-hot. Then, with pulleys, they brought it under the power hammer. It works with incredible precision. The workers repeated the operation several times before obtaining the exact form the engineers wanted.

"I have a friend who works at the iron works. The heat is so unbearable that he has to wear special padding and gloves. He even has a mask to keep his face and eyes from burning.

"But do you know what, Louise? What I find so amazing is the way in which the power hammer works. It's powered by a steam engine and its precision has been regulated within a fraction of an inch. It weighs one hundred tons and is capable of corking a bottle without breaking the spout. I even remember when an engineer took off the cover of his watch and put it under the hammer. The hammer closed the cover and hardly touched the watch."

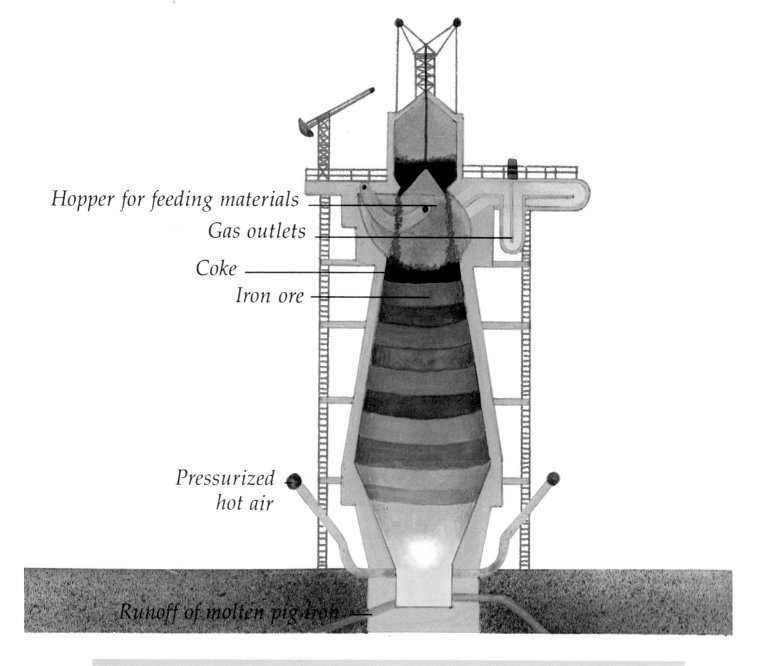

Hopper for feeding materials

Gas outlets

Coke

Iron ore

Pressurized hot air

Runoff of molten pig iron

The Blast Furnace

The blast furnace is a stone tower almost 100 feet tall, surrounded by a pipe through which hot air is blown. The inside of the furnace is lined with firebricks that resist heat up to 3600 degrees Fahrenheit. When a new blast furnace is put into production, a worker smashes the bricks at the bottom of the furnace and makes a hole through which the molten pig iron can flow. The blast furnace operates day and night, nonstop for more than ten years.

Building Metal Monsters

Gustave and Louise walked for several hundred yards and came to another building. This was the building where guns, wagons, locomotives, and many other kinds of machines were made. Huge metal arches held up the roof with its large glass windows that let more light into the workshops. When they came near an assembly workshop, they were able to see some huge objects under the arches. They were newly-built locomotives.

Railroad tracks led into the huge workshop. Wagons went back and forth, bringing the separate parts to the assembly points. Each one of the locomotives being built weighed 80 tons. The workers assembled each one, piece by piece, like a huge jigsaw puzzle. The teams received orders from a supervisor. The workers had to take extra care not to lose or damage any of the parts. If they did, they might have to pay for it!

Emile, Louise's other brother, worked on an assembly line. He and his companions put the wheels on the locomotives. There were four small wheels and four big ones. The small wheels were linked to one another by axles. The big wheels were called driving wheels because they were powered by the steam engine and made the locomotive move. The steam engine, along with the boiler, cylinder, and pistons, were the last parts to be assembled and put on a locomotive.

Emile left the workshop after a hard day's work and walked over to Gustave and Louise. He picked up his little sister and whirled her around in the air. They both broke out laughing. As he put her down Emile said, "Here is our future teacher!"

"Oh, don't jump the gun, Emile. Wait until I've finished studying!"

"Hello, Gustave," Emile said as he returned Louise to the ground. "You look beat! Working at that blast furnace is killing you."

"I think maybe you're right. It's wearing me out. But you look in great shape."

"Really, I like what I'm doing at the moment. We're building a magnificent locomotive. If everything goes as planned, it should reach a speed of 80 miles per hour. Can you imagine? I can't wait to see it go."

"How much horsepower does it have?" Louise asked.

"Well, little sister," Emile said with a smile, "I must say, you seem to know an awful lot about horsepower!"

"Of course I do! We had a lesson on it last week. I can even tell you how a steam engine works! The boiler in the train's engine is filled with water. Underneath there is a firebox with a grate. Coal is burned on the grate and heats the water. As the temperature of the water rises, steam is let off. The steam goes into cylinders and pushes the pistons. These are connected to rods that make the big driving wheels turn."

"And would you mind telling me why the engine's power is measured in horsepower?" Emile asked.

"That's easy. You can measure the force of a horse pulling a certain weight over a certain distance and in a given time. Are you following me?" Louise asked, very proud of all she knew.

"Not exactly, but go ahead," Emile answered.

"I'll give you an example. It's been figured that it takes a horse one second to pull a 550 pound load two feet. That is how horsepower is determined. If your locomotive has 100 horsepower, that doesn't mean that there are 100 horses in the boiler. It means that your engine can pull 550 pounds multiplied by 100, which is equal to 55,000 pounds two feet per second.

"Very good, Louise! Next week you can tell us what it means if the locomotive has a 300-horsepower engine!"

From the *Rocket* to the TGV

Richard Trevithick built the first steam locomotive in 1804. Earlier attempts to use steam power for transportation purposes had been made in France in 1769 and England in 1785. George Stephenson, an Englishman, built his first locomotive in 1814 and the *Rocket* in 1829. The *Rocket* could travel at 15 miles an hour. England became the first country to build train engines on an assembly line. In the late 1830s steam locomotives came into general use to pull passenger and freight trains.

After 1850, progress was made quickly. In 1890 a locomotive (also built in England) went over 85 miles per hour. Later on, the use of electricity made it possible to obtain even better speeds. In 1903 a German locomotive reached 125 miles per hour.

Since 1981 the world record for speed has been held in France by the TGV (*Train Grande Vitesse*, which means "high-speed train" in French), with a speed of 228 miles per hour.

The Strike

As evening approached, fog slowly covered the small town. Only a faint outline of the blast furnace and the factory chimneys could be seen. Even sounds seemed to be muffled.

Louise and her two brothers found their way home in the damp evening air. Emile and Louise had stopped laughing. Now they all continued on in silence. All three had the feeling that something strange was going to happen that night. The feeling became stronger when they reached the coal-mining town.

Small groups of people were gathered in front of many of the homes. Their faces showed signs of worry and concern. Louise, Gustave, and Emile kept hearing a word repeated. Just one word, "strike!"

When they arrived at the town square, they met their mother. Before any of them could ask what was happening, Jeanne said, "The miners have gone on strike! This morning they would not go down into the mines because of last night's accident. Your father and other miners met with the director of the mine. It didn't go very well! They're now meeting to decide what the next move will be. I am going to join them."

"Is Father a representative?" Louise asked.

"Yes, he's part of the group that has been elected by the miners to represent them."

"We're coming with you," Emile decided. "Louise, you can continue on home, if you like."

"No! I want to come, too."

Voices could be heard coming from the meeting hall. A heated discussion was going on. People were yelling and shouting. Louise, her two brothers, and their mother silently slipped into the room. Their father came to greet them.

"We went to see the director of the mine just before noon," he told them. "We told the director that we had had enough. We refused to work under such harsh conditions without any safety precautions or decent wages. We told him that the timbermen were forced to use old wooden beams to prop up the galleries. With conditions like that, the slightest cave-in was bound to result in a serious accident. Antoine was killed! He had just turned seventeen! The director didn't even listen to us. He won't negotiate until we go back to work. We're determined to stick it out."

Paul was shouting more than he was speaking. He spoke of the miners' misfortunes, hardships, and sufferings.

"No one will go down tonight or tomorrow or the day after! We'll hold out until the end! If we want justice, the only way we can get it is by going on strike."

"On strike!" Louise thought. She remembered the last strike. She had been only six years old at the time. For two months she felt as if she were living in war time. Soldiers had been sent in with orders to break up even the smallest sign of a gathering.

"Father," she said with concern in her voice, "if you go on strike, there'll be hard times, won't there?"

"We'll manage. Over the past year we've been putting money into a relief fund. Every two weeks the miners have given a small part of their wages in case of strike. We didn't think it would happen this quickly. But, that's how things go!"

To reassure his daughter, Paul took her by the hand and walked out of the room. Outside, night had fallen. It was dreadfully quiet. It seemed as if a storm was about to break on the town.

May 1st

When the first factories appeared, there were no laws to limit the number of hours people had to work.

For years, the working class in Europe and the United States organized itself and fought to reduce the number of hours spent working. Strikes and demonstrations were common. On May 1, 1886, a meeting in the United States turned into a riot. Five workers were arrested and sentenced to death. In 1889, in remembrance of these events, May 1 was declared an international day of protest for workers.

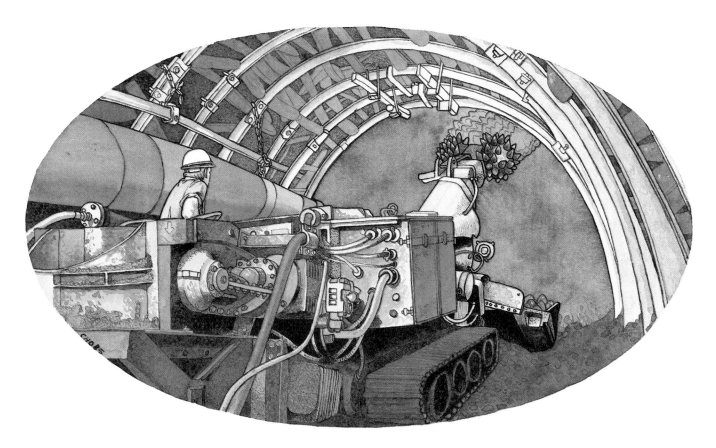

A modern mining machine digging coal from a gallery

Mines of Today

Today, coal mining is a highly mechanized industry. It is much less difficult than in the past. Galleries are dug by machines and supported by metal or concrete rings. The coal is removed from the seam with a coal-cutting machine. This machine is like an enormous chain saw. The coal is transported on conveyor belts and dumped into buckets, which are brought to the surface.

Nowadays, many mines are open-pit mines. This makes it much easier to remove coal.

Places to Write for More Information

You can find out more about coal-mining and the steel industry today by writing to the associations and companies below. Ask them to send you copies of their educational and promotional information.

American Iron and Steel Institute; Communications and Educational Services Department; 1000 16th Street, N.W.; Washington, D.C. 20036

United States Steel Corporation; 600 Grant Street; Pittsburgh, Pennsylvania 15203

National Coal Association; 1130 17th Street, N.W.; Washington, D.C. 20036

Pittsburgh Coal Mining Institute of America; 4800 Forbes Avenue; Pittsburgh, Pennsylvania 15213

Miners digging for coal (from a sixteenth-century engraving)

Important Dates

Around 1000 B.C.—People discover how to forge iron
1600s—First underground galleries built for extracting coal
1710—English iron maker Abraham Darby first uses coke to smelt iron
1765—Scottish engineer James Watt develops steam engine
1856—Bessemer Converter produces low-cost steel
1890—United Mine Workers of America union founded
1906—Mining disaster in Courrieres, France, kills over 1200 miners
1936—France passes law providing paid vacation time
1969—Federal Coal Mine Health and Safety Act passed by Congress
1975—"Robotization" introduced in mining industry